"PAX & PERRY'S AMAZING DAY AT THE ZOO"

BY

TRINA C. BASS

ZOO

What a bright and sunny day for a new adventure just minutes away! Pax and Petee enjoyed the morning sun. They sat back and waited for their new day of fun!

This brother and sister duo were at it again. Yearning for the doors to open at the zoo for their new journey to begin.

At 9 o'clock on the dot the doors were opened. Pax and Petee ran fast with a hand full of tokens. With no words spoken, the two continued on their stride without it being broken.

The zookeeper shouted, "Hey you two kids please stop running!"

With two big smiles they stood and said, "We can't! We can't! All of the amazing animals are coming!"

So away they went to see their first zoo animal, but not before the brother and sister saw a few things that were laughable.

The monkeys were the first animals in sight. They swung on trees and played at very great heights. Eating banana after banana it made their bellies feel pretty tight.

Before Pax and Petee's imagination could begin, all of the monkeys fell asleep causing it all to end.

They were not sad about the sleeping monkeys you see, their sights were now set on the elephants near the trees.

The brother and sister stood in shock at the elephant's great size. In their minds within minutes those huge animals became just a little larger as they blocked the sky.

Their imagination took them to a prehistoric time which turned the elephants into Mammoth's right before their very eyes.

This prehistoric creature had fur and a long curved tusk. It scooped them up onto its back as they all headed towards the corn husks.

With a heavy stride and a bumpy ride they headed towards the deck, to visit the animals with a much longer neck.

The giraffe you see was very tall and covered with lots of spots.

Then suddenly it became a Brontosaurus with a small head, whip-like tail, slightly shorter forelimbs, and eyes that looked like dots.

Being one of the largest prehistoric animals to have ever walked the earth. With its large long neck and huge appetite for plants which probably started at birth.

Pax and Petee were having an amazing time at the zoo with their new friends the Mammoth and the Brontosaurus 'tis true. Now it's time for something with a much different hue.

The crocodile was next in line. With its grayish green color and narrow long snout design.

    Pax and Petee sat on the Mammoth with the Brontosaurus in tow. They watched the crocodile covered in dirt before swimming in a pool of water preparing for a muddy show. As it dipped back under the water out of sight it turned into a Spinosaurus in broad daylight.

The Spinosaurus was the world's first swimming dinosaur without a doubt. With its small pelvis, short hind legs, as well as long and narrow snout.

"You're our friend now Mr. Spinosaurus," said Pax and Petee.

Mr. Spinosaurus replied, "I'll come and join you but I'll try not to be greedy."

Having an unusually long and narrow skull with needlelike teeth made eating for this prehistoric animal pretty easy.

Now that the Mammoth, Brontosaurus, and Spinosaurus are on the zoo tour, it's time to see something new, something different but Pax and Petee were unsure.

They all filed in a straight line looking for the next zoo attraction to see. It was the Komodo dragon inside the reptile cage near the humming black and yellow bumble bees.

The Komodo dragon is the world's largest living lizard with its long forked tongue. It has been using it to smell and taste ever since it was young. With its scaly skin and little ear holes it began crawling near the red poles.

Within the blink of an eye and a slight turn of their neck, in the minds of Pax and Petee this Komodo dragon had now become a Tyrannosaurus Rex.

This prehistoric reptile had Pax and Petee grinning. With wide opened eyes and a beaming smile these two were really winning. By mentally creating a Tyrannosaurus Rex out of a Komodo dragon, their imagination was definitely not lagging.

The Tyrannosaurus Rex, also referred to as the T-Rex, had a massive skull and a heavy long tail. With its small powerful arms, and two clawed fingers it walked on its hind legs.

Pax and Petee invited the T-Rex along, to see the next animal with them while gently humming a song. The Mammoth, Brontosaurus, Spinosaurus, and Tyrannosaurus Rex were on their way to see the final animal of the day.

The tiger stood covered with stripes. Playing with its baby cub while blocking it from the sunlight. It roared as Pax, Petee and friends came by but suddenly stopped at the twinkle of an eye.

The tiger, who once was a tiger, was a tiger no more. Just like that, it became a prehistoric Saber-toothed cat! This primitive cat had a mind of its own with its long upper teeth and deep widely arched cheek bones.

It jumped over the fence ready to play with Pax, Petee and the rest of the gang. It jumped around then sat back down while showing its mighty sharp fangs.

Pax and Petee shouted, "C'mon you guys we're headed this way! There's so much more to see and we don't have time to play."

Away they all went with Pax and Petee taking the lead. The Mammoth, Brontosaurus, Spinosaurus, Tyrannosaurus Rex, and Saber-toothed cat were all marching in the breeze.

The Polar bears, Panda bears, penguins, parakeets, lions, and Gorillas were a hop and a skip away. The zebras, Rhinos, Llamas, and kangaroo were also seen today, HOORAY!

Their prehistoric journey was now complete. After the zoo was preparing to close, they were heading home for some relief.

After a big day of dreaming for this brother and sister with happiness in their eyes, it was time to rest and tell all the animal's goodbye.

FUN LEARNING ACTIVITIES
For
PAX & PETEE'S
AMAZING DAY AT THE ZOO

1. Unscramble the words
2. Fill in the blank
3. Wacky Word Search
4. Big Word Vocabulary
5. Find the missing letters
6. Multiple choice questions
7. Use your imagination like Pax and Petee to draw your very own picture

UNSCRAMBLE THE WORDS

1. GERTI   _____

2. IRGAFFE   _____

3. DILECROCO   _____

4. PHANTELE   _____

5. KEYMON   _____

6. DOMOKO GONDRA _____

7. KEETPARA   _____

FILL IN THE BLANK

1. Pax and Petee are sister and _____.

2. Pax and Petee love to have fun at the _____.

3. They rode on the _____ as they went on their zoo tour.

4. In their minds the zoo animals became prehistoric _____.

5. The monkeys ate too many _____ which made their bellies feel tight.

WACKY WORD SEARCH

Find the following words:

1. MONKEY
2. TIGER
3. ZEBRAS
4. LION
5. LLAMA
6. ZOO
7. BEAR

Z	Y	E	K	N	O	M
E	T	K	O	L	O	L
B	I	B	O	I	D	L
R	G	E	Z	O	G	A
A	E	A	E	N	P	M
S	R	R	H	O	U	A

BIG WORD VOCABULARY

1. Define the word prehistoric?

2. Define the word Mammoth?

3. Define the word Brontosaurus?

4. Define the word Spinosaurus?

5. Define the word Tyrannosaurus Rex?

6. Define the word Saber-toothed cat?

7. Define the word Komodo dragon?

8. Define the word lagging?

9. Define the word primitive?

10. Define the word reptile?

One answer is given...

1. Tyrannosaurus Rex: A large meat eating dinosaur that walked on two legs.

FIND THE MISSING LETTERS

1. Mam_oth

2. _ron_osaurus

3. Sp_no_aurus

4. T_ra_nosaurus R_x

5. Sa_er – t_othed C_t

MULTIPLE CHOICE QUESTIONS

1. Pax and Petee went where _____?

    a. to the zoo   **b.** to the playground   **c.** shopping

2. Pax and Petee daydreamed about _____?

    a. food   **b.** dinosaurs   **c.** cars

3. Pax and Petee hopped on top of the _____?

    a. the mouse   **b.** monkey   **c.** mammoth

4. Pax and Petee were daydreaming of _____ animals at the zoo?

    a. cars   **b.** prehistoric   **c.** bananas

USE YOUR IMAGINATION LIKE PAX AND PETEE TO DRAW YOUR VERY OWN PICTURE

Made in the USA
Columbia, SC
26 January 2018